To: Nancy

From: Sheenie

Hate

Hatla I got in
a book and on
TV !! !
° °
Sheenie

MCSWEENEY'S BOOKS
SAN FRANCISCO
www.mcsweeneys.net

826

THANKS AND
HAVE FUN RUNNING THE COUNTRY

Kids' Letters to President Obama

EDITED BY JORY JOHN

WHEN BARACK OBAMA WAS ELECTED to the presidency on November 4, 2008, a portion of San Francisco's Mission District—specifically Valencia Street—erupted into a spontaneous celebration, resulting in the closure of a few blocks, while a thousand people circled around each other in a human whirlpool of joy, hugging strangers, climbing poles, hollering from apartment windows. There was actual dancing in the streets. Parents came out with their children. The police showed up, but they hung back and watched, cordoning off the area, making sure folks were safe. There was a lot of energy, but it was peaceful and respectful, the way it would feel if everybody around you was on the same page about everything and knew it. It had been totally organic, building from a few people, whooping at cars from the sidewalk, to a giant outpouring of emotion. You simply wanted to bask in it.

Directly adjacent to that night's gathering is a nonprofit writing and tutoring center, 826 Valencia, where I serve as the programs director. One of my duties is coordinating the after-school tutoring program where, every day between 2:30 and 5:30 p.m., about sixty kids from the neighborhood stream into our lab (located directly behind a pirate-supply store) to get help with their writing and homework. The students range in age from six to eighteen, and when they arrive, they quickly take over the space, and the room transitions from serene to vibrant. It's my favorite time of day.

"FIRST!" the first kid, almost always a student named Adrian, will exclaim when he arrives. Shouts of "second!" and "third!" rapidly follow (I suppose we could be flattered that it's become a competition to get to *tutoring*), and, soon enough, the homework is removed from backpacks and volunteer tutors are assigned to their student(s) for the day. The parents often stick around, some sitting on a converted church pew at the front of the room, near an actual redwood tree that's bolted to the floor for atmosphere. Kids take breaks and venture over to my desk to tell me about the latest movie they saw, whose birthday is approaching, or how my shoes are outdated and lame. Homework is completed. Snacks are distributed. The kids choose a book to read. And then, it's writing time, usually for the last hour or so. This hour is open for interpretation, whether the students want to create a story, a poem, a screenplay, a comic strip, etc. We publish many books and there's always an outlet for their work.

About a week after the election, I had an idea: why not have the kids put their thoughts to President Obama down on paper, bind them into a homemade book and send them to the White House? At the very least, it could be an engaging exercise, getting the students to think about the new president's challenges and goals. I asked for everybody's attention one day, and made my pitch. Various kids nodded in assent. No one yelled "No!" This was a good sign. We proceeded.

As I collected the letters, I realized that this idea had hit a nerve. Everybody had something personal and different to offer the president, whether it was advice, or stories of their own lives, or funny ideas, or special requests. We got in touch with our sister chapters—the other 826 centers around the country—located in New York, Boston, Chicago, Ann Arbor, Seattle, and Los Angeles, and we asked if they'd get their students to write letters, too. Everybody was excited about the idea and we waited to see what would happen.

Directors and tutoring coordinators moved quickly, and the results were incredible. Many of the letters were hilarious, filled with very specific questions ("Do you have to pay bills?"), or offering unusual advice ("I would fill the White House with chocolate and gravy…"). But there were also a number of letters that were extremely heartfelt. You'll find some truly amazing writing in here from all seven cities, as kids take the opportunity to tell President Obama their dreams of a better life in America and specific ideas of what they'll need along the way.

Consider this: many of the kids included in this collection have only known one presidential administration in their lifetimes. So this is an incredibly exciting moment for them. Given that most of our students are from heterogeneous backgrounds themselves, they definitely feel ownership over the whole idea of an Obama presidency.

I've loved seeing the kids participating, writing, wanting to be heard, believing that President Obama will listen to *them*. Here's hoping that the act of writing their letters to the president will translate into engagement as young adults, and continued participation in their neighborhoods, their country, and beyond.

Jory John, Editor
January, 2009

The best
Precedent

Marco Ponce, age 10, San Francisco

"I know you want to save the earth, but people don't want to clean."

Dear President Obama,

I know you want to save the earth, but people don't want to clean. My life is to clean up all the world and help you to clean. I always dream of cleaning the world with you. I'll do anything for you because you are the president in this world.

Stephanie Gonzalez, age 7
Los Angeles

"Look around the White House. Meet with your helpers. Get a puppy. Talk to America. Make a speech. My name is Matthew Wong."

Dear President Obama,

The first thing you need to do is put your stuff in the White House. Be careful, Abraham Lincoln haunts one of the bedrooms. Look around the White House. Meet with your helpers. Get a puppy. Talk to America. Make a speech. My name is Matthew Wong. I am eight years old and go to Skinner School in Chicago, IL. I like my school because it is big, but I have problems with my homework. I was watching TV when you were elected. My family was happy.

Can you stop pollution? It kills people, plants, and animals.

Sincerely,
Matthew Wong, age 8
Chicago

"Something happened to me: I went out to lunch at Starbucks and I wanted to buy a cup of whipped cream and normally it's forty-three cents, but now it's seventy-four cents! The price raised thirty-one cents for no reason."

Dear Barack Obama,

I voted for you! I think you really will make a difference to the United States! My name is Alexis Feliciano, I am nine years old. I go to school at P.S. 321 William Penn School.

One thing you could fix is the economy. Something happened to me: I went out to lunch at Starbucks and I wanted to buy a cup of whipped cream and normally it's forty-three cents, but now it's seventy-four cents! The price raised thirty-one cents for no reason. So you should probably try to change things like that from happening. You should keep an eye out for things like that.

I wish you good luck! I trust you! And also, I believe you could change the United States!

P.S. I love whipped cream!
P.P.S. Write back!

Love,
Alexis Feliciano, age 9
Brooklyn

Dear Obama,

You are going to be a great president. My whole religion voted for you. I am happy that you are going to be our present. Because you are going to do great stof for th U.S.

I wanted to tell you that I am arabic and I heard that you were half way arabic. I think that you deserve to be the president becaus you were going to do smart and good stof, like give poor people homes and a life.

to Obama

from Bushra

Age 8

Pittsfilde elementary

Bushra Habbas-Nimer, age 8, Ann Arbor

Dear Obama family,

When you move into the White House, turn on the heater so it won't be cold. You could also take hot baths in your new antique bathtubs. Or you could make hot tea and coffee.

When I moved to a new house, I helped my dad. He took apart a chair and I carried pieces of it. If I were your helper when you move in, I could move everything!

Have a nice day being the first family.

Nazrawit Dessie, age 7
Seattle

"If I were president, I would help all nations, even Hawaii."

Dear President Obama,

Could you help my family to get housecleaning jobs? I hope you will be a great president. If I were president, I would help all nations, even Hawaii.

President Obama, I think you could help the world.

Chad Timsing, age 9
Los Angeles

"I'd have a couch made out of pudding that you could eat with a giant spoon. After we'd eaten all of our furniture, we'd buy real furniture."

Dear Mr. Obama,

As president, I would move into the White House and get some people to help me with my homework. I would fill the White House with chocolate and gravy (but not together) and mashed potatoes or maybe fill it with root beer. I'd drive through the White House on a boat. We'd make the floor out of mashed potatoes and the house would be filled with mashed potatoes. When visitors from other places come, I'd tell them to eat mashed potatoes and drink the root beer through giant straws. I'd give out cotton candy and food to the people and feed them dinner.

I'd have a couch made out of pudding that you could eat with a giant spoon. And I'd have a pizza carpet. After we'd eaten all of our furniture, we'd buy real furniture.

Amir Abdelhadi, age 6
(as dictated to Katie McCaughan)
Chicago

Dear President Obama,

I hope you enjoy reading my letter. I would like to start by introducing myself. My name is Chandler Browne, I'm twelve years old and attend Pritzker School in Chicago. In my letter, I'm going to give you some advice. I think I would like to give you advice about the war in Iraq. People there are dying (but I'm positive you already know that). You should get the troops out (but I'm sure you already know that too). Also, settle the war.

Now some advice for your family, and specifically, how you can find a dog: I understand that Sasha is allergic to animals with fur. Well, my dad is allergic too, and I have some suggestions on what breed to get. Here are some dogs you can get: Cockapoo, Labradoodle, and Goldendoodle. I hope you take my suggestions into consideration.

Here is a list of the first ten things you should do as president:

1. Fly to the White House in a helicopter.

2. Walk in.

3. Wipe feet.

4. Walk to the Oval Office.

5. Sit down in a chair.

6. Put hand sanitizer on hands.

7. Enjoy moment.

8. Get up.

9. Get in car.

10. Go to the dog pound.

Finally, I would like to tell you where I was when you were elected: I was about 250 yards away from the stage you spoke from on election night. I was so excited when I found out that you were going to be president. Please enjoy your experience as president.

Sincerely,
Chandler Browne, age 12
Chicago

Giselle Perez, age 11, San Francisco

Dear President Obama,

Whatever happened to McCain? If I made up a rule, it would be to have snow cones every week. You should give the whole United States of America snow cones. No, your servants should do it. It's easier. I wish I could get an autographed picture of you.

Sincerely,
Hamza Saalim, age 8
Ann Arbor

Dear President Obama,

What will you do in the White House? I learn in school every day, but people don't listen, like David. We need to learn in school. You could help me to multiply all the numbers. You could help my friends play catch. You could help my family make a project of a dinosaur. If I were the president, I would make people houses.

Obama, what are you doing in the White House? What are you going to do in the White House?

Anthony Vasquez, age 7
Los Angeles

Dear President Obama,

I believe you will do marvelous things for our country. As a thirteen-year-old, I'm confident that I could make a list of ten things I would do if I were the president. But I'm not. So here's a list of things *you* should do as President of the United States.

1. Health care for everyone!!!
2. Eat a donut (or two).
3. Play with your family.
4. Buy donuts for your family.
5. Read the book *Elsewhere* by Gabrielle Zevin.
6. Pass a law to allow gay marriages in all states.
7. Ban the right to bear arms.
8. The right of freedom of speech should be modified.
9. Limit the sale and consumption of alcohol and tobacco.
10. Modify the budget for schools in North America.

I have the determination to pursue the dream to be the president.

Sincerely,
Heaven Willis, age 13
Chicago

Giselle Perez, age 11, San Francisco

Dear President Obama,

When you are president, don't eat junk food. Junk food makes you fat. Your family shouldn't eat junk food, either, because it is not healthy.

Obama, you rock.

Amy Ramirez, age 8
San Francisco

Dear Barack Obama,

Congrats on becoming the President of the United States and slaughtering John McCain. I think that, unlike W., you should dodge other countries and not shoes. You should not be so quick to go to war and negotiate with terrorists.

I like what you said about bringing the troops home from Iraq. If you like my letter, know that it's from:

D'andre "The King" Legrand, age 12
Brooklyn

Dear Mr. Obama,

My name is Lydia and I am ten years old. I am from Seattle, WA. My favorite thing to do is to read and my favorite book is nonfiction. It is about horses and how to ride.

I am very happy you were elected president. I love your speeches. My friends and I looked on the computer when you were doing your speech.

I was wondering what kind of dog you are getting? I think you should get a Labradoodle and name it Soñador (it means "dreamer" in Spanish).

I hope you can change our state and the United States.

From,
Lydia Sumner, age 10
Seattle

"If I want anybody to be president, it's me."

Dear President Obama,

If I want anybody to be president, it's me. I would clean the streets and give myself more money. I would also give everybody a piece of a Reese's candy. Every homeless guy or girl would get $50 for help and a place to sleep for the winter. My family and other families would get free gas for our cars; single people with no kids would have to pay.

The money would come from copying other bills. The $1, $2, $5, $10, $20, $50, and $100 bills would be copied one thousand times.

The paper would not come from trees, but hardened glue. The way to make it is by mixing water and glue together so that it looks like paper. You then put it in a fire, then let it cool in the freezer.

Weslie Jackson, age 12
Chicago

My name is Petra I have 7
years old my school is Edison
Charter Academy

my advice to my President
Obama is not to forget us
to give money for schools
and prowgrams were we go
for help to do our
homework. And help poure People

Merry chrismas Obama!

Petra Cardoso, age 7, San Francisco

To President Obama,

If I were president, I would help the people. If we don't throw the trash away, we are going to get sick. I could walk around to check where there is trash.

From,
Kenia Zelaya, age 6
Los Angeles

"I think it is great to have a black man as president. You sound like an interesting man."

Dear President Obama,

My name is Gabe Honeycutt and I live in Seattle, Washington. It's a nice city, but it rains a lot. I like *Spider-Man* comics, too, and my favorite music is jazz. I've been to Hawaii and it was very hot there. Do you miss living there?

I think it is great to have a black man as president. I think you could have won even without Mr. McCain's help. You sound like an interesting man. You stepped up and helped people. I wish you could help the homeless people here in Seattle by making the non-used hotels into shelters.

I'd like to see more parks in our cities and fewer apartment buildings going up everywhere. Maybe you could lower the prices for health care, especially for people who can't afford medicine and are dying because they don't have it.

Hope you and your family like it in the White House.

P.S. Don't get a rat dog. I think a mutt would be great.

Thanks for listening,
Gabe Honeycutt, age 9
Seattle

"You come up
with good ideas?
Nothing?
It's fine."

Dear President Obama,

Why did you volunteer to be president? I like your good ideas. Don't let the USA down.

You come up with good ideas? Nothing? It's fine. It's all fine.

I did a screenplay. It was made into a movie by the Echo Park Film Center and people working with me.

I will do everything you say. You're nice and persuasive. You are one of the good presidents.

Alex Morones, age 10
Los Angeles

Dear President Obama,

I want to tell you hi. Do you work with Santa Claus?
Can I meet you in your house? Can I say bye to you after
I meet you? And then can I meet you again? And then
again after that?

Sergio Magana, age 5
San Francisco

Dear Barack Obama,

You are one of my friends. I cannot believe you are president. In our community, you're the best guy I've ever seen. You rock the whole world. I cannot believe you did such an awesome job.

Love,
Jennifer Navarreto, age 10
Brooklyn

MR. OBama

Diana Perez, age 10, San Francisco

Dear President Obama,

I noticed that the financial crisis is changing lives. So I think you should stop it, somehow, because families are getting poor. It would be helpful to the USA if you did this. Instead of a hero, you would be a superhero.

You and I both want change, because every single time a Republican is picked as president, they always do the same thing as the last one.

Your faithful constituent, I am,
Khaled K. Hamdan, age 11
Brooklyn

Giuseppe Pacheco, age 7, San Francisco

Dear President Obama,

I want a gasoline card. I need the gasoline card because me and my family are going to Yosemite Valley, but I want to save a little money. We will buy food for my family. One hundred dollars will be enough.

Obama, can you come visit Echo Park? I like Los Angeles because it is not like Mexico City. I like the servants in the White House. If I was president, I would give all the money that I make to the poor.

Edgar Lucas, age 11
Los Angeles

"You are just
like a big me."

Dear President Obama,

You are just like a big me, because I am from Chicago and I am biracial and have curly hair. I live in Seattle now, but I'm still from Chicago.

How do you feel about being president?

I have an idea. Why don't you give everybody, even the homeless, ten dollars every day? Each person would need this money for food, clothes, toys, and many other needs. And don't forget to give the kids money, too.

My advice for you and your family is be yourself and you will change the world. If I were president, I would try to make the world a better place.

Sincerely,
Avante Price, age 7
Seattle

Dear President Obama,

Do you have to pay bills?

You are brave because I am very shy in front of people, and you talk to a lot of people. Most of all, the best part of being in the White House is you have your own guards!

From,

Rachelle Hull, age 10
San Francisco

Dear Mr. Obama,

When you're the president, Obama, you should change the world and make new rules like no littering and no guns around, Christmas joy, and no smoking. This is some good advice to the first African-American president.

If I were president, I would make the world change and make it a better place to live. I would make it fair, like make everyone be nice and listen to people, and respect them, too.

Khaya Monteiro, age 8
Boston

Dear Barack obama

I'm glad you won to be Presondent my family vote for you your family is so proud of your even your wife and daughters or sons and could you please help us with the war.

by Amanda Lee Sosa

Amanda Lee, age 8, Brooklyn

Dear Mr. Obama,

Hi, my name is Marco, and I live in San Francisco. I am ten years old. I am writing this letter because I want to stop the war in Iraq and make the economy better. This is important because a lot of people are getting killed shooting at each other. Families are sad and worried about losing their loved ones. Also, the war is very expensive.

Mr. Obama, you should send the troops back to America. We can use the money saved to heal soldiers, and build schools for kids with low incomes, and help families with their needs. Thanks, Mr. Obama, for reading my letter about my problem. I like you being my president. I wish you good luck and to be elected again.

Sincerely,
Marco Ponce, age 10
San Francisco

Dear President Obama,

I would like to know if you could fix the economy and the war problem. How would you avoid shoes being thrown at you? And why did you choose the Democratic Party? Also, why do you think no other African Americans ran for president?

From,

Edgar Laczano, age 11
San Francisco

Dear President Obama,

My name is Kevin. I have one brother and one sister
and their names are Anthony and Dayanara. My favorite
food is soup and my favorite breakfast is cereal. My
favorite fruit is a pear and my favorite thing at the store
is Hot Cheetos.

Sincerely,
Kevin Romero, age 7
San Francisco

"You should also build cameras all around our city to find out who is breaking the law. We also need to save the forest."

Dear Barack Obama,

I have some comments about things going on in this place. You know, we really need to have some new cars to save our environment. We also need to persuade people to stop smoking—you can let people buy one more pack, but that would be their last pack. After that you have to stop selling cigarettes. You can have a little bit of beer, but not too much—don't go wild or anything.

You should also build cameras all around our city to find out who is breaking the law, and also in movie theaters so we can tell who is making illegal copies. We also need to save the forest. Another thing that you should do is that for all the people who are out there asking for money, you should help them get into college. That way those people can teach their kids, instead of being homeless.

> **Ray Crespo**, age 12
> Boston

Dear President Barack Obama,

First of all, I am very happy you were elected president. When I was watching television on November 4, I started crying because I was so happy. Everyone in my neighborhood kept honking their cars, yelling, and texting their friends about how you had been elected the forty-fourth president. My friend's dad is going to open a new ice-cream store right in front of my house and they are going to try to open it on January 20 in honor of you. :) My family and I have been talking about when you become president it is going to be very hard for you because of the economy. Don't worry, you have me, my family, my friends, and St. James School to support you.

I have some questions, and I really would love for you to answer them back. OK, here they go. How will you help all the US immigrants? How will you help us students in our education? Will you try to make the U.S. a more environmental place? Well, those are my main questions.

I just want to say that you are going to be a great president and don't worry about anything, just remember that you have two wonderful daughters that love you and a wife that loves

you too and remember that she is as beautiful as a rose.
I hope, Mr. President, that you don't do the same mistake
as Mr. Bush about the war. If we want peace in our world,
we must at least start somehow. We end up getting so mad
about how we want peace in the world when we end up
making hate.

My dream is to become a veterinarian or a zoologist because
I love animals and I think I will get more connected to our
planet. I have dreams that I want to achieve that are why my
parents, my brother, and I immigrated to the United States
with our American Dream. My neighbors think that I am just
another Latino that is going to ruin her life. But they are so
wrong. I want to go to great high schools. I want to graduate
from college and show my mom that I worked my butt off.

Well, thanks, and I hope you have a great time running
the country. :)

Sincerely,
Yoselin Teresa Martinez Xonthe, age 13
San Francisco

"If I were president, I would tell people to not talk too much. It wastes time."

Dear Mr. Obama,

If I were president, I would tell people to not talk too much. It wastes time.

I would give the poor people more money so they don't have to look for food in the trash can. I would also give them a house. I'd work really hard so I could buy them a house and give them more food.

If I were the president, you wouldn't have to pay rent. When you go to the store, you wouldn't have to pay for sure!

I'd also say to war: no more, no more, no more!

Catherine Galvan, age 6
Chicago

Giselle Perez, age 11, San Francisco

Dear Barack Obama,

I have a great idea for you: you should set up a special phone, a special place just for kids to call the president if they find things that are dangerous and can affect people, like someone smoking. This would be a special place for kids to talk to Barack Obama and let him know what's going on.

Another important thing that I want to talk to you about is cars and buses. There is a bus called the Galactic Wizard which runs on biofuel or vegetable oil. I think instead of polluting the environment, scientists should work on those buses. You should make it so that everyone turns off any light whenever they are not in the room—that way we can save the environment and also pay less on our electricity. We can't just use up the environment until we have nothing, or we will starve to death. Nobody wants that, do they? I want to tell you, Barack Obama, if one day I could travel around the world and help people, I would definitely do it.

Dhamaril Nunez, age 9
Boston

Dear Obama,

If you were going to make up a holiday, what would it be?
If you were going to make a law, what would it be? I liked you
before you were even president.

I'm friends with Jerey Best, the girl that was on CNN and also
sent you a letter.

Sincerely,

Lauren Solomon, age 11
Los Angeles

Dear President Obama,

I think that this year you will have to do a lot of work. One thing that you will have to do is to make school more important for everyone. That way kids will always do a good job.

If I were the president, I would work really hard to change Boston and other cities. I would make the world very smart. I would make all of the world work really hard and always do the best job that they can.

Gabriela Quezada, age 7
Boston

Giselle Perez, age 11, San Francisco

Dear President Obama,

First of all, let me congratulate you on your job. I like that you are the first African-American president and that you made history. Obama, I would say to you and your family: don't spend a lot of money on Christmas. Oh, and don't raise taxes. I will be writing to you again. And my teacher said she will probably write to you saying come to our school. Please come. It would be nice. Bye!

Sincerely,
Jason Lee, age 9
Los Angeles

"What stuff is in the White House?

Answer here:

_____ "

Dear President Obama,

What is your favorite holiday? My favorite holidays are
Christmas and Halloween. I would be a good president and
stop bad drugs. What stuff is in the White House?
Answer here:

_____

You would never say bad words because you would never
break the law.

                    Sincerely,
                    Kevin Cordova, age 7
                    Los Angeles

"I wish I was your long lost son."

David Muñoz
Age 9

School St. Charles

Dear Mr. Obama Please Take care
of your Family. Bring your Family
Peace.

1   First you should Bring peace to the
    World.

Second Thing you should Do is stop The
wars.

Third Thing you should DO is stop
The killing.

I live in San Francisco it's a good
place But it's too cold. it is
too violent.

I would like to live in white house
Because you have a cool
hot tub. also I would have a
comfy Bed. your Friend
David. PS I wish I was your
long lost son

David Muñoz, age 9, San Francisco

Dear Mr. Barack Obama,

My name is Madison, but everybody calls me "Madi" (or "crazy," it depends on who you ask). I'm eleven years old, almost twelve, and I'm in the sixth grade. I'm very happy for you, your wife, and your daughters. Also, I'm glad that you are the president. At first, during the election, I really wanted you to become the next President of the United States of America. After a while, though, I realized that I thought differently.

I decided that as long as whoever won helped the USA and the rest of the world, I was good. I really hope that you are that person who changes history for the better.

My family and I were rooting for you since the beginning. We watched several of your speeches. Everybody in our house was very happy when you won the election. America needs change and we all think that you're the man for the job. My dad, my mom, and my little brother all wish you well.

I have some advice for your daughters: I know that it's hard to move and leave your friends behind; when I was five my family moved from Seattle to Pleasanton, California. I remember that it was sometimes hard for me there, but I think it was mostly the dramatic temperature change.

My advice for Malia and Sasha is to just be yourselves. Don't worry about making friends. Just talk and socialize and you'll figure out who you like and who you don't. It might seem hard at first, but it all turns out fine.

I hope that you settle into the White House and enjoy your presidency. I also hope that Michelle and Malia and Sasha all adjust OK.

Sooooo... what are you going to name the puppy?

Best wishes and good luck,
Madison "Madi" Rupp, age 11
Seattle

Dear President Obama,

If you could lower gas prices, it would be good so people could not waste their money. Or if they waste all their money, they should have more chances before they become homeless. This country should be the richest. If you could do this, people in this country would not be homeless.

So lower gas prices.

Jackson Huang, age 10
Los Angeles

Dear President Obama,

Hello! Since I know you, I thought it would only be fair if you knew some stuff about me. My name is Gabby, I am thirteen years old, and go to Pritzker School in Chicago. I like to listen to music and make lists. So I will list the first ten things you should do as president.

1. Sit down.
2. Get a glass of water.
3. Use the bathroom.
4. Wash your hands.
5. Take a nap.
6. Look around your new house.
7. Eat something edible.
8. Converse with your family.
9. Cough…
10. Whatever else you feel like doing at the time.

It's really great that you got elected and I'm sure you'll do great in office. So, have fun. I have to end this letter somehow, so…

In awesomeness,

Gabby Rozenberg, age 13
Chicago

Jennifer Muñoz, age 10, San Francisco

Dear Obama,

My name is Stephanie. Even though you may not listen to me, I want to tell you what's important for my family and me. Lowering the prices on expensive things is one of them because sometimes we can't afford things. For example, we can't afford a house of our own. I wish you could put more money in schools because a lot of kids are leaving schools. More money would be good because we could get more materials for school. I like your idea of stopping the war because it's dangerous. When my cousin was in the war I was really worried. Less people would die if the war *stopped*.

I want to know how it feels not having any privacy, everyone knowing how old you are. I would like to live in the White House because servants could do everything for you. It would be fun because you could run all over the house and hide so no one could find you. I would *not* like to be president. You know why? Because everyone would know your personal things.

Sincerely,
Stephanie Aguilar, age 10
Los Angeles

Dear President Obama,

You should make a three-day weekend. Give the homeless a home. Make renting less money. Let people have free pets. Make a free-money day.

Sincerely,
Emily Morales, age 9
San Francisco

Dear President Obama,

If I were president, I would take every single drug off the streets. I would also take out all homework. Instead we could do everything in class. Also, I'd keep the environment cleaner and with less bad people. Also, I'd keep the market prices lower.

When you were a candidate, I wanted you to win and you did! I wish everybody could have more money. My favorite holidays are Christmas and Halloween.

Also, have you won any medals?

Jessica Cordova, age 10
Los Angeles

Mr. Obama

Diana Perez, age 10, San Francisco

Dear President Obama,

My parents went door-knocking for you in October. The first thing you should do when you take office is create better working conditions, especially for the AFL-CIO. The AFL-CIO was in all battleground states helping you.

I think schools should have better food. I'm sick of micro-waveable burritos. YUCK!!! You have inspired many of my friends and convinced many people that race doesn't matter. Please, please, consider all of the above!

Sincerely,
Sky Parkhurst, age 12
Los Angeles

Dear Mr. Obama,

Hey, I'm Sheenie, I'm kinda a poet. I really hope you put America back together. No pressure though. I bet you get a lot of admiring letters from your millions of fans, but I hope my letter is special enough for your eyes to travel to the end. I'm not much of a political follower, but I know people like me suddenly got interested. I heard you on the radio, I saw you on TV, your face was cool and confident, but what stopped me was the eloquence in your voice. The voice that was made for a thousand speeches.

One day my mom went to the library to find one of your books. What was annoying and miraculous at the same time was that the book had sooooo many holds. I think we waited two months for it.

I'm thinking maybe you're the kind of person who doesn't like to be treated like a king. Maybe you want to be an ordinary person again and you can walk out in the street without someone screaming with delight at the sight of you.

I also want to talk to you about the problems in America, the economy, and of course the war. You promised, I think, to fix it, and I believe you're a person who keeps a promise.

To your family, they might be excited, yet stressed, for the first days in the White House. I'd think you'd not be ready to fix those huge problems yet. Sit down, get a nice, icy glass of water or whatever you find refreshing, forget your powerful duty, and be an ordinary man that just got off a long plane ride. Malia and Sasha, help your dad, give him strength, determination, and will.

I might be able to write to you all day long and the funny thing is, I don't even know you. You really are just the confident figure on my TV screen, ready to take on a nerve-~~wracking~~ _WREAKING_ job. I might see you in the rarest of chances, but then again you would just be a smiling, waving figure, maybe shrouded with your bodyguards.

I have hope in you, Mr. Obama, and I hope this letter gave you a little piece of happy-reading joy.

Sheenie Shannon Yip, age 13
Seattle

Dear President Obama,
My advice to you is really nothing because I beleive that you can CHANGE the U.S.A.. I am so happy you are our president

♥ Much Love,
chanel

Chanel Jones, age 10, San Francisco

Lydia S.

Dear Mr. Obama,

My name is Lydia and I am ten years old. I am from Seattle, WA. My favorite thing to do is to read and my favorite book is nonfiction. It is about horses and how to ride.

I am very happy you were elected president. I love your speeches. My friends and I looked on the computer when you were doing your speech.

I was wondering what kind of dog you are getting? I think you should get a Labradoodle and name it Soñador (it means "dreamer" in Spanish).

I hope you can change our state and the United States.

From,
Lydia Sumner, age 10
Seattle

"The best thing about living in the White House would be running around like a maniac."

Dear President/Mr. Obama,

Please stop global warming. Try to make natural gas out of water, or a car that can use waste as fuel because we're going to run out of gas.

The best thing about living in the White House would be running around like a maniac. The thing I would like least is the work.

P.S. You might want to do more charity work, fundraisers, and giving to the homeless. Please give the money to schools, families that need it, and people who live on the streets.

Holly Wong, age 9
San Francisco

Dear President Obama,

First of all, thanks for overcoming such a big feat. I am eleven years old and a true Obama fanatic! My name is Henri Fitzmaurice and I live in Seattle, Washington. I have worked at your phone banks all around Seattle. I have lived in Seattle since I was born in 1997. I am an actor and love performing in musicals. I am hoping to audition for a play this spring.

One of my concerns is drought. My grandmother lives in Berkeley, California and, like Seattle, it rains a lot! But at her summer home, just thirty minutes away, there is a big drought. I think that whoever becomes your Secretary of Defense should make droughts a big priority. Not just in the USA but in other countries, too.

The economy, it is bad. Almost every day we reach a new low. Back in the "happy" days, Americans were buying bigger cars and SUVs. Then gas prices soared up to four dollars a gallon. People thought they were being wiser by putting their big cars in the garage for a while. Ever since then, the gas prices have gradually trickled down. Now people think that the worst is over, and they are now taking out their SUVs and they're driving them like they did before.

I think, and many other people think, that the worst is not over. The Dow Jones is down. A couple of years ago, that was nothing. Now people are losing their jobs because of that. I was reading a newspaper headline on November 1, and in the month of October, Americans lost 240,000 jobs.

I believe that you can fix the problems in Iraq and Afghanistan, and I believe you can solve the unanswered questions about the economy and global warming.

I believe you can succeed and, Barack Obama, I hope you do.

A true fan,
Henri Fitzmaurice, age 11
Seattle

Dear Obama,

I would like to congratulate you for being the next president.
I heard your speech and read it from the newspaper and
liked it. Your speech was amazing. I saw many signs saying
"Vote 4 Obama '08." Some people said John McCain was
going to win. But I knew you were going to win. I hope you
write back so I could know more about you.

Sincerely,

Carlos Luna, age 12
San Francisco

Dear Obama,

I like you because you won. We saw you on TV. I hope
I am your friend.

Sincerely,
Edwin Martinez, age 6
Los Angeles

name: Alysha
8 years old
Rooftop School

Dear president Obama,

My name is Alysha.
I play the piano. I'd played the piano
for three years! My dad owns two
restraunts. My dad and Mom works at
Fresh Green. My dad is the boss, My mom
is the assistant.
Some advice I'd want to give you
would be to take care of the
environment. I care about animals. and
would like to see their homes
protected. Your daughters should stay
intouch with their old friends.
I hope you make the world a
better place.

Sincerely,
Alysha

Alysha Chen, age 8, San Francisco

Dear Mr. Obama,

My name is David Gonzalez and I'm nine years old. I go to Brighton Elementary School and I am Cuban, but I was born in America. Cuba is a very nice country, but I don't like the weather because it is so hot. Seattle is very cold. I like it when it's snowing.

I like to play basketball and kickball and I like to swim.

Maybe you could help places where adults help the younger people with their homework. Also, places like Bike Works, where instructors teach kids how to fix and ride their bikes safely. Also, they ride to places with kids.

Global warming also affects us. We could make more natural cars. We could plant at least one tree in everyone's yards to clean the atmosphere. To clean the earth, we must do a lot.

Sincerely,
David Gonzalez, age 9
Seattle

Dear Mr. Obama,

I wish you could give me money and buy me a Nintendo DS and a DS game. Mr. Obama, are you rich? Don't cut more trees down, because I have hard homework.

I know you can be a better president than President Bush.

Vote yes on Obama!

Sincerely,
Giuseppe Pacheco, age 7
San Francisco

Dear Barack Obama,

I want to talk to you about college scholarships. There are a lot of people who don't go to college because they can't afford it and they can't get scholarships.

You should cut all public colleges' prices. You should create a scholarship for people who write three pages about what they want to do with their life. My friend Mike, who is twenty-one, didn't go to college because he can't afford it. He would be able to get the scholarship.

Could you give me a full scholarship to a college in Seattle?

Danny Giday, age 13
Seattle

Dear President Obama,

Congratulations! Do you think, when you are president, that you could equalize sports for both genders? In my school there was a wrestling team only for boys, even though some girls wanted to try out for it. Only the boys got to get in. I feel it's kind of sexist, and I think that you inspired people by becoming the first African-American president, so you can try and show that everyone should be able to do whatever kinds of sports they want.

Good luck for the next four years. I was glad that you became president, and I believe in you.

Your future leader,
Laura Marshall, age 11
Brooklyn

Dear President Barack Obama, *Renea*

I'm Renea. I'm nine years old. I go to school at Greenwood Elementary School in Seattle. I'm a straight-A student. I like art and math.

I think you should focus on education, global warming, and the wars.

Education is important so kids can get jobs like you did and so they can get the right amount of change when they go to the store because people use math every day. Without school, people would just sit around and watch TV all day. There should be more art in school—plays and stuff— because creativity is important.

Global warming is bad. As president, it would help if you helped create more park-and-rides and public transit, like trains and bike-sharing programs. Also, wars are unhelp- ful—I think you should stop them, if you can.

Good-bye,
Renea Harris-Peterson, age 9
Seattle

Dear President,

I think people should stop polluting and stop animal cruelty.
That's my advice. I think you're going to be a good president.
I think you should most importantly take care of your family.
I think you should stop war because a lot of innocent people
are dying in the war. Stop war, stop pollution, stop animal
cruelty and try to stop global warming. Those are some things.
There's global warming because people pollute. That's not
nice. Just think about the penguins and the polar bears and
all the animals that live in the ice.

Sincerely,
Oscar Miranda, age 10
Los Angeles

Sophia

Dear Mr. Obama,

Hi, my name is Sophia Mandell. I live in Seattle, Washington and I go to Salmon Bay School. I'm ten years old and in fourth grade. I have two older brothers: Aaron, fourteen, and Jacob, sixteen. I also have a dog. I love school and sports. I play baseball, basketball, and soccer. Also, I like snowboarding and swimming.

Something my family and I would like to ask you is: what are you going to do about the war in Iraq and the war in Afghanistan? I hope you can stop them. What I would do is try to get a meeting going and have some people from both countries and have them talk to each other and try to solve their problems with words.

Maybe you could also try to lower gas prices. Talk to the owners of gas stations and see if you could get them to lower their prices and tell them they will still get paid a lot of money. It will help the environment and people will not have to spend so much money on so little gas.

Well, I hope you do a good job!

Sophia Mandell, age 10
Seattle

President Obama,

You should not smoke when you are president! There are simple reasons. Because you will die by smoking, and then you will not be president! But I want you to be.

Your number-one fan,
David Lopez, age 7
Los Angeles

Dear President Obama,

I am ten years old. I am a nice girl and I like to write. I wish you could be the first president of all the world. Obama, when I went trick-or-treating on Halloween, people were giving me candy and telling me to vote for you.

Obama, I think it will be better if you tell the people that sell TVs, and all those things, to sell them for a lower price because my mom and my dad are not working and not getting a lot of money. I want people that are not in a house and don't work to get something for Christmas.

Obama, if I were president I would change a lot of things in this world.

Paulina Rojas, age 10
Los Angeles

Giselle Perez, age 11, San Francisco

Dear Sir Obama,

Would you please make cars powered by water?

You should read *Here's a Penny, Two and Two Are Four,*
Betsy and Billy, Back to School with Betsy, Primrose Day,
and *Penny and Peter,* all books written by Carolyn Haywood.

These are the first ten things you should do as president:

1. Make everyone read books.
2. Don't let teachers give kids hard homework.
3. Make a law where kids only get one page of homework
   per week.
4. Kids can go visit you whenever they want.
5. Make volunteer tutors get paid.
6. Let the tutors do all the thinking.
7. Make universities free.
8. Make students get extra credit for everything.
9. Give teachers raises.
10. If number-four is approved, let kids visit the Oval Office,
    but don't make it boring.

Sincerely,
Mireya Perez, age 8
San Francisco

"You could give biscuits to the dogs and yarn to the cats."

Dear President Obama,

My name is Rosie Barrantes. I'm in the fifth grade at Rooftop School, in San Francisco. I'm ten years old and I love animals. I love animals because they are very kind and beautiful. I have a farm/rancho in Mexico, where there are calves, puppies, dogs, cats, kittens, horses (and their babies), hummingbirds, nests with baby birds, donkeys, and foals.

Could you help all the animals in the shelters because animals need love and care? Dogs and cats are sometimes hurt and get hit by cars. Or people leave them without food, water, or shelter and sometimes put them in fights. I have an idea that maybe you can donate food and water to the dogs and cats in the shelter. You could give biscuits to the dogs and yarn to the cats. Maybe if you know anyone who loves dogs and cats, they can go to the SPCA and give the animals care, love, shelter, food, and water. That's how I think you should change the world.

P.S. What are you going to name your dog? You should name him Max. That's from *How the Grinch Stole Christmas*.

Rosie Barrantes, age 10
San Francisco

Dear Mr. Obama,

Hello! My name is Justine Cameron. I live in Seattle, Washington, and I go to Washington Middle School. I am eleven years old. I think that I am very different from all the other people that you have ever met (and I am guessing that is a lot of people). I love singing, dancing, and acting. I am in a play called *Oliver Twist* at Broadway Bound (that is a kids' acting company) and when I grow up I am going to be a musical actor.

I know that you have a lot of work to do with the United States and I think that you could use some help. That is why I am writing this letter.

The United States of America is a very interesting place. There are millions of people doing tons of stuff all of the time. There are so many people that sometimes there are problems. Schools have problems. And I am particularly interested in education.

My school is a very good school. We have a good curriculum, a very good music program, and wonderful sports. But the neighborhood has a lot of crime. Almost every week, we have

Justine Cameron this page ↓

a lockdown. (A lockdown is when there is a crime happening around the school and we have to lock our windows, close the shades, and lock our doors just to be safe.) It is really scary and everyone gets really freaked out.

I hope that you can help us make our neighborhood, and all neighborhoods, safe. Maybe you can make sure that everyone has enough to eat, wear, and a place to live. Maybe you can reward people for good behavior? I am not sure what to recommend, but I think that everyone should be able to be safe when they go to school and all schools should be good schools.

Well, good luck finding a dog, too. (I love dogs.)

Sincerely,
Justine Cameron, age 11
Seattle

Dear President Obama:

You are awesome!!! Some things you should do are:

1. Stop the use of oil in cars.
2. Clean up the ocean.
3. Help animals that are endangered.
4. Help immigrants get better jobs.
5. Give money to schools.
6. Fire the governor of California.

Love,

Hilda Herrera, age 12
San Francisco

Mr. President,

Obama, change the world. Change the world by making new laws, like no throwing trash on the streets and no guns around—that way people won't die. You should put the bad people in jail, and change the teachers from screaming at the students to working hard.

Change the universities to make them better so that students can all learn math problems. And change the street rules, like make sure people do not drive so fast when there's a red light.

You should split up the FBI and make more police. Also, don't make any wars because the innocent people are going to die that way.

Angel Edwards, age 8
Boston

Emily Morales, age 9, San Francisco

Dear President Obama,

I would like you to help my family by bringing the rest of my family from El Salvador to the United States. If they come, you could give my family jobs and also make them citizens.

Sincerely,
Alanis Gordillo, age 10
Los Angeles

Dear President Obama,

I really want to congratulate you for being our new president.
I hope you can make a change because I saw all those posters
that said "Vote For Obama For a Change." If I were president,
I would look back to you and see what you did.

What I would like to see you change is the prices on products.
My family needs help with everything: health care, insurance,
and making schools affordable. I want to be able to go to
college in about four years.

My name is Miguel Villalobos. I'm in eighth grade and I go to
St. James School. We need a change. We can do it! We are the
United States of America.

Miguel Villalobos, age 13
San Francisco

Dear President Obama,

These are the most important things you should do:

1. Let Latinos come to America.
2. Stop the war in Iraq because so many innocent people are dying.
3. Please help stop global warming by making electric cars cheaper.
4. Help people pay for their houses by lowering taxes.

Carlos Ramirez, age 11
San Francisco

Dear President Obama,

I want to meet you at my tutoring program with my teacher, Bonnie. Did you ever go to a tutoring program after school like me? What age are your daughters? Are they eleven years old like me? Are you going to help people like my parents find good jobs?

I want to tell you that I learned to ride my bike. That is good because I get exercise and play with my friends. It would be cool if everybody rode bikes because they don't use gasoline and they don't make the air dirty. If I were a president, I would give people jobs.

Furthermore,
Karla Mora, age 11
Los Angeles

Dear President Obama,

Be a good president. I voted for you because you are nicer than the others. Me and my family think you are more helpful than McCain. Obama, if I were a president I would copy the same things you are doing because you are helping people who are from Mexico.

Good luck, President Obama, on being a president. I am happy you are the new president. Obama, my sister is intelligent and so am I. I like to play my Nintendo DS.

We are working hard for you. You are more intelligent than the others.

Sincerely,
Citlali Mora, age 9
Los Angeles

Dear Mr. Obama,

My name is Daniel and I am twelve. I live in Seattle, Washington and go to Asa Mercer Middle School. I am in sixth grade. My most favorite thing to do is to BMX. I hope you have BMXed before. If not, you should try it, because it is very fun. I go to Bike Works and learn to fix bikes. It's a really good place here in Seattle.

I really hope you can help with the crime problem and the violence that there is in my neighborhood. I live on Rainier Avenue and there are many crimes, like shooting and a lot of stealing. I had a beautiful Siberian Husky named Michael that was three years old and when I was working with my mom someone stole him. I was very sad. My brother David and I were crying.

I wish I was older than twelve so I could find a job and help my family since we are poor. My family is from Cuba, even though I was born in the United States. I have gone to Cuba three times. Cuba is very different than the USA because in Cuba you don't get to choose the religion you want to do.

My family left because we are Jehovah's Witnesses and our lives were in danger. In Cuba, there are not any big cities and the people live on farms or close to the woods and there are animals that eat the crops and other animals and we must protect them. Most houses are made of mud and old wood. The best ones are made of old metal.

Also, the schools are waaaay different because only the best ones might have a roof.

I congratulate you and thank you.

Sincerely,
Daniel Gonzalez, age 12
Seattle

"Martin Luther King Jr. had big fans. How many fans do you have?"

Dear President Obama,

Are you going to be pictured on our money? How do you
get in the White House? Do you like Abraham Lincoln?
Do you have a big backyard? Martin Luther King Jr. had
big fans. How many fans do you have? You could help us
by giving us food. I am Luis Ramirez. I go to school at
Mayberry. I like to play video games.

Luis Ramirez, age 8
Los Angeles

Dear President Obama,

You are the coolest president in the world and you help people and you love them. If I were president I would do the same things as you.

Javier Morales, age 9
Los Angeles

Dear President Obama,

We have some advice for you: take care of immigrants who don't commit crimes because it's not their fault that they are immigrants. Also, they try very hard to stay in this country because this country has lots of jobs that get paid very well. Also, our economy is not well, so we will really appreciate it if you could help our economy get higher. Also, stop the war with Iraq because they are getting very poor. Why are we fighting Iraq? And why are we involved in every war that happens?

We wanted to invite you to Edison Charter Academy, San Francisco, CA. It's near Dolores Street. Thank you very much for reading our letter. We hope you will visit our school and tell us more about you.

Sincerely,
Jennifer Muñoz, age 10,
and *Giselle Perez*, age 11
San Francisco

Dear President Obama,

You are cool. I saw you on the TV and you beat John McCain. You are a great president for Los Angeles and you are a great president for the United States.

You rock for me, Obama.

Love,
Bryan Rojas, age 8
Los Angeles

Dear President Obama,

My life in San Francisco is good. My parents have good money, I go to a good school, and people in San Francisco are happy that you are president. Because you are a new president, I advise you to help the economy because every day on Wall Street is another unsuccessful day. I would like you to give money to schools, poor people, orphanages, and sponsors to kids. Lower taxes on people who earn less than $200,000 a year. Make more schools with good education for kids who don't have much money. I want you to tell car companies to produce more hybrid cars so we can save the environment and gas. Stop the factories from making aggregates, and other unhelpful drugs.

I would like to live in the White House because I would have private rooms, chefs, gardens, baths, swimming pools, parks, and beds. I wouldn't like living in the White House because you wouldn't live a normal life, and I would be lonely.

Congratulations, President Obama!

Sincerely,
Kalden Ritschel Auleatsang, age 10
San Francisco

Dear President Obama,

I am so glad that you are the next president! If I could sit down with you, I would tell you that you should stop global warming. Also, I would tell you to give food to poor people because some of them are dying for food, clothes, and water.

I would also tell you to help sick people and give them health insurance. And last, I would tell you to have a great time being president and living in the White House.

Ambar Arredondo, age 10
Los Angeles

Dear President Obama,

I am so happy you are our new president. If I was eighteen or older, I would've voted for you. That's for sure. I think that the first thing you should do as president should be to help immigrant people. They come for a better life and they want their kids to have a better education and better opportunities. I know it's not that easy but I think that you could help them with their dreams. I also think that you can help with the economic problems.

One thing that I would like you to know about my life in San Francisco is that sometimes it can get difficult, but it's fun to live in a very cool city. The thing that I would like most about living in the White House is that I would be living in a very famous house. Well, I think that it's not possible to not like living in the White House.

All the best,
Dolores Cervantes, age 12
San Francisco

"I think you should get a lot of rest and eat healthy because you have a really big job commitment for this."

Dear President Obama,

I have some advice for you. Please make this world a better place. I say this because we want no more war. We also don't want jobs to be gone because then we will be left with no money and no food to eat. We want no guns or violence on the street because they have killed many innocent people. I think you should get a lot of rest and eat healthy because you have a really big job commitment for this.

Sincerely,

Edgar Gomez, age 11
San Francisco

Dear President Obama,

Could you help me because I have trouble paying my bills?
You should give me money because we don't have money.

How are you? I feel good in Los Angeles.

Jesenia Reza, age 8
Los Angeles

Dear President Obama,

You will be a great president. I wish you could change the world. If I were president, I would give people tickets to go to different places in the world. Or you could sell them for not much money. I wish I could be in the White House with you.

Sincerely,
Martha Romero, age 10
San Francisco

Dear President Obama,

I'm in seventh grade and attend Aptos Middle School.
I am in the journalism class and because of journalism's
ties to politics, the projects our class hosted during the
election really showed me how the children of this
generation understand politics and view the world. Our
class held a mock election for the school and we are
making a film about the election and the world. We
interviewed our fellow students and one of the questions
we asked was, "How do you want the world to change?"
At least two-thirds of those answers were related to
peace and the stopping of the Iraq War.

Another question was, "Who did you vote for?" Everyone
said "Obama." When asked why, we were given such
answers as "Obama is trying to raise taxes on wealthy
people and that is fair because poor(er) people don't have
that much money."

I hope this shows you that my age group gets a bad rap.
Adults often assume our opinions aren't valid because we
repeat the opinions of our parents. It may be true that
children raised in more Democratic households will lean

more towards the left while children brought up in Republican environments will lean to the right. This, however, does not mean that our opinions about politics and the world are not our own.

On the day after you were elected as the next President of the United States, something had changed in all of us. I think it was the thing that you endorse: hope. Throughout the day people would whoop and holler and call out your name. This was genuine joy, not the mirror reflections of our parents' feelings.

You should realize that not just the adults of the nation are watching you, that the younger generation is too. And while our parents may have learned to stay silent as the world is not fixed and our leaders do things to benefit themselves—we, most definitely, will not.

Sincerely,
Giorgia Peckman, age 13
San Francisco

"It was very enjoyable writing to you like this, President Obama."

Dear President Obama,

My name is Eli Mrozek. I'm ten years old. I live in Seattle, Washington. I am the oldest child in my family. I have one sister named Mahala. I have two dogs named Maggie and Roger. My favorite series of books is *Harry Potter*. It's the best series in the world! Now that you've heard about me, I want to give you ideas about how to make our country prosper.

I need to bring up a huge problem, the economy! I have a chain of events that you could trigger to lower the economy. First, get a green design company to design a new environmentally safe piece of technology. Then, create new jobs to install the new piece of technology. Finally, from the new jobs people will have more money, there will be less homeless people, which will end in a better economy.

I am very lucky to be writing to you like this. I hope you enjoyed my idea for a better country. It was very enjoyable writing to you like this, President Obama.

Yours truly,
Eli Mrozek, age 10
Seattle

Dear Obama,

I hope this letter reaches you in the best of health and condition, following your victory in the presidential race.
I figured I'd share my opinions on the White House. Most of all, the White House is a very historical and honored place. Living in such an environment must feel a little different and weird. I guess the best thing about the White House is the experience of being there for a term or two terms and really sucking everything up, be it good or bad.

Sincerely,
Mohammad Jama, age 14
Ann Arbor

INDEX

ACKNOWLEDGMENTS

Eliana Stein, Nínive Clements Calegari, Dave Eggers,
Teri Hein, Amanda Uhle, Joel Arquillos, Leigh Lehman,
Scott Seeley, Mara Fuller O'Brien, Daniel Johnson,
Eli Horowitz, Brian Gray, Joan Kim, Deborah John,
Inez Machado, Avery Monsen, Toffer Lehnherr,
Julius Diaz Panoriñgan, Danny Hom, Bonnie Chau,
Pat Mohr, Miranda Tsang, Jenny Traig, Jordan Bass,
Walter Green, Leora Silverman Fridman, Kait Steele,
and all of the kids who participated: many thanks.

San Francisco
WWW.826VALENCIA.ORG

Los Angeles
WWW.826LA.ORG

New York
WWW.826NYC.ORG

Chicago
WWW.826CHI.ORG

Ann Arbor
WWW.826MICHIGAN.ORG

Seattle
WWW.826SEATTLE.ORG

Boston
WWW.826BOSTON.ORG

826 NATIONAL

826 National is a family of nonprofit organizations dedicated to helping students, ages six to eighteen, with expository and creative writing at seven locations across the country. 826 chapters are located in San Francisco, Los Angeles, New York, Chicago, Ann Arbor, Seattle, and Boston.

Our mission is based on the understanding that great leaps in learning can happen with one-on-one attention, and that strong writing skills are fundamental to future success.

Each 826 chapter offers drop-in tutoring, field trips, workshops, and in-schools programs—all free of charge—for students, classes, and schools.

826 is especially committed to supporting teachers, offering services and resources for English-language learners, and publishing student work. All locations offer unique retail experiences as well.

To learn more or get involved, please visit
WWW.826NATIONAL.ORG.